Basics and Fundamentals of Computer Information Systems

by

Dr. Alfonso J. Kinglow

CONTENTS

CHAPTERS

DEDICATION

I want to dedicate this book to my wife Sarah for her support, dedication and kindness and to my
Grand children
Kenney, Anaiah, Karmelita, Kahlil and Kalysha, who I wish one day will read my Books and be challenged and Inspired to seek Knowledge and Wisdom, and to Explore.

" Knowledge is Wisdom, and Wisdom is Power; let it be kept from fools, who may use it to do evil ."
Siddhartha

"If any of you lack wisdom, let him ask of God, that giveth to all men liberally, and upbraideth not; and it shall be given him."
KJV - James 1:5

PREFACE

With this book I want my readers to understand the basics and fundamental parts of a computer system as they relate to either Business Information Systems and Computer Information Systems, or just a basic Computer; it is written for Basic users, Seniors as well as Advance users.

And to engage and educate students and readers, and give them all the information they will need to investigate and obtain in depth knowledge of the Windows built-in Software and Utilities how they work and perform, that they can use, and challenge them to think and explore, and be inspired as they read my books.

The basics will consider both Terms and Acronyms and the fundamentals that deal with Laws, Rules, Regulations, Conditions, Protocols and Standards that govern the basic information, the bit; the smallest unit of information, a binary number that represents zero (0) or (1) the binary computer language of a computer, to process information.

As we consider the fundamentals, the classic example is the Internet that uses both Standards, such as ANSI or Defacto Standards and Protocols, like the World Wide Web (WWW), the TCP Protocol combined with the IT Protocol to produce the Internet Standard, TCP/IP that is required for Networks to communicate.

We should consider the Rules for Networks to work correctly, using the OSI Model (Open Systems Interconnect) a Networking Model Standard, and the Rule of 30, one of the many Rules in Computer Technology.

CHAPTER ONE

CONDITIONS and RULES

The basic Rule of 30 says, that for every 30 minutes of continued computer work, where your eyes are focus on the video display screen; you should raise your head and look about 30 feet away, from where you are; for 30 seconds, to avoid and prevent Eye Fatigue and Headaches when using a computer. This is just one of the many basic rules used in Computer Technology.

Conditions in Computer Technology:

Negative and Positive conditions in Computer Information Systems (CIS) and Business Information Systems (BIS) .

NEGATIVE CONDITION:
Don't use:　　I Think......................
　　　　　　　I Believe …..............
　　　　　　　Maybe …..................
　　　　　　　It could be …...........
　　　　　　　Perhaps …...............
　　　　　　　 Is it? …...................

POSITIVE CONDITION:

Use or Say: I KNOW.............
                    IT IS …..............
                    I DONT KNOW ..
                    IT IS NOT …......

Users of Computer Systems should use:

 Critical Thinking ---------- Analytical Thinking

 Logical Thinking --------- Conditional Thinking

To resolve issues with Computer Information Systems.
Computers are TASK DRIVEN Machines, which is different from The Human Basic Information Process.

Machine and the Human Basic Information Process

Computers are Task Driven Machines that contain the ALU, or Arithmetic Logic Unit or sometimes called the "Motherboard", and consist of Input, and Output. The Input is the Keyboard, Mouse, Tape, Microphone, etc.. and other devices used to enter information into the computer. The Output is the Monitor, or Video Display, the Disk, a Flash drive, Tape recorder, etc..

The ALU contains the OS (Operating System), RAM

Random Access Memory, ROM Read Only Memory, PROM Programmable Memory, The CPU Central Processing Unit, MOM, Microsoft Operations Manager and DAD, Data Access Devices.

All of these constitutes the basic Machine Process; which also includes: Rules, Laws, Analytical Data Processing, Statistical Data Processing, SPI's Supervised Parallel Inputs and SPO's Supervised Parallel Outputs.

The Machine Process can use Pure Mathematics, Empirical and Imaginary Numbers, Standards and Protocols, and Analog and Digital processes to obtain results, for a given Task.

The Human Basic Information Process

Humans process information by using Critical Thinking, Conditional Thinking, Logical Thinking, Analytical Thinking, Comparative Thinking, Multitasking and Reasoning. This can be done all at the same time; this makes us different from machines., and very unique., when we want to obtain results.
 It is therefore important to understand how machines process information., so we do not ask machines IE. Computers, for information that they can not provide or understand, and have to display a **404 Error,** or as it was done in the old days of IBM Computers, where the user would get a message that said: DUMMY, CAN NOT DIVIDE BY ZERO (0).

Built-in Tools in Windows Computers

USER TOOLS

Most Windows Computer Operating Systems (OS) will have two types of Tools Built-In and some of them hidden from the user. They are external User Tools that the user can obtain FREE on the Internet to keep their computer Clean, and Protected from Viruses and other Malware.

At least three (3)areas of the computer must be kept clean, to enhance performance and to protect both the Hardware and Software.

These areas are: The Registry, The System, The Hard Drive. Other areas are optimized as well with these user tools. The Tools are:

- ADVANCED SYSTEM CARE 10.4
- GLARY UTILITIES 5.76
- ACEBYTE UTILITIES
- CLEAN MASTER
- MALICIOUS REMOVAL TOOL
- THE ADVANCE FOLDER (Create from CODES)
- THE ALL APPLICATIONS (Create from CODES
- WIN PATROL EXPLORER
- WIN PATROL HELP

SYSTEM TOOLS

The System Tools are:
- ANTIVIRUS
- WINDOWS FIREWALL
- WINDOWS DEFENDER
- MICROSOFT MANAGEMENT CONSOLE
- COMMAND LINE CMD
- WINDOWS SHELL COMMANDS
- MICROSOFT PHONE
- MICROSOFT PHONE COMPANION
- EXPLORER SHELL
- DIAGNOSTIC TOOLS
1. PERFORMANCE MONITOR
2. RESOURCE MONITOR
3. SYSTEM CONFIGURATION
4. RUN
5. TASK MANAGER
6. NARRATOR
7. PRINT MANAGEMENT
8. SYSTEM INFORMATION
9. UNINSTALL
10. WINDOWS FIREWALL WITH ADVANCED SECURITY
11. WINDOWS MEMORY DIAGNOSTIC
12. DXDIAG DIAGNOSTICS

WINDOWS BUILT IN DIAGNOSTIC TOOLS

To access the Diagnostic Tool DXDIAG, right -click on the Windows startup icon, in the lower left side of the screen, to display the "**RUN**" command.

Type inside the RUN command: **DXDIAG** and press <Enter>.

The Diagnostic program will start to run and check all of your machine. Follow the screens. " No problems found" will be displayed " if your computer is ok.

The Diagnostic Tool will detect any problem your machine may have.

THE ADVANCED FOLDER IN WINDOWS

The Advanced folder is created from hidden CODES in Windows., for fixing and troubleshooting all parts of the computer.

Create the **ADVANCED. FOLDER**

Then type the CODE exactly, with OPEN and CLOSED Brackets like this **{   }** and not this **[   ]**

Start:

1. Create a New Folder
2. Give it a name: ADVANCED.
3. Put a period after the D.
4. Enter the CODE exactly:

Advanced.{ED7BA470-8E54-465E-825C-99712043E01C}

<Enter>

A new **Green Folder** will be created on the Desktop containing 237 Files Tabulated and in order, with graphics, showing where, when and why to Fix and Troubleshoot all parts of the Computer.

WINDOWS MICROSOFT MANAGEMENT CONSOLE (MMC).

On the Startup or RUN command, type: **MMC**
The Microsoft Management Console Window will be displayed, showing the Console root.

Follow instructions on this Window to create **" Snap-ins"** to Manage any part of the Computer. A Step-by-step Guide is available on the Internet, on how to do this, or available at the end of this book.

CHAPTER TWO

THE BASIC COMPUTER SPECS.

The Basic Computer Desktop or Laptop will have a CPU from INTEL, that is Dual-Core i-3, i-5, i-7 or i-8 with a speed of 2.5 GHz, 3.0 GHz or higher. Intel Processors are recommended.
The Memory or RAM (Random Access Memory) should be a minimum of **4 Gigabytes** (GB) or **8GB** is preferred.

Memory should not be 3GB or 6GB found in some computers. This type of Memory configuration is unacceptable, as it is sharing the user memory with its video. Standard Memory Configuration is always 1 GB, 2GB, 4GB, 8GB, 16GB, 32GB, 64GB, 128 GB., etc..

The Computer should have at least 4 USB Ports; (Universal Serial Bus) to connect external devices and supports version 2.0 and the new version 3.0 Standard and one HDMI Port. (High Definition Multimedia Input) Port.
The Hard Drive (HD) Storage (c:> drive) should be a minimum of one Terabyte (1 Tb.)

The Internal Wireless Network Adapter Card should be **802.11/AC** the new Standard, or a minimum **802.11/n** which is slow, less than 100 Mb per second, the Ethernet Standard.

The internal fixed Ethernet Adapter Card should be one gigabit (1 GB) Gigabit Ethernet., for higher speeds.

The Microsoft Operating System should be 64 Bit OS using Windows 10 basic edition or the preferred, Pro Edition or Windows Pro. They are still 32 bit computers in the marketplace, but 64 bit computers are best. The OS must match the computer 64 bit version or the 32 bit version.

The minimum Video Display should be 15.4 inches or 17 inches for a larger display, supporting high resolutions.

The preferred Computer brands are: SAMSUNG, SONY, LENOVO, HP, ACER, TOSHIBA, ETC..

The computer should have a built- in CD/DVD R/W Drive to play CD and DVD Music and Video. The DVD should be a Read/Write or R/W to enable recording a blank CD or DVD.

INSTALLING MICROSOFT WINDOWS 10

Windows 10 was released July 29, 2015 and it was FREE for 1 year if you have Windows 7 or 8.
Get a FLASH DRIVE of 8 GB. Insert it into one of the USB ports on the computer.
Download Windows 10 " Content Creation Tool" Select to Install Windows 10 Home if you have Windows 7 select to install Windows 10 Pro if you have Windows 8 or 8.1

Run the " Content Creation Tool " 32 bit or 64 bit
Install on the 8 GB USB FLASHDRIVE. Then,
Install Windows 10 from the FLASHDRIVE on the Computer that is being upgraded.

NEW WINDOWS 10 INSTALLED

The new Windows 10 contains a new Browser called Microsoft "EDGE", a new Personal Digital Assistant, called " CORTANA", and support for the new Standard USB Port version 3.0

Windows 10 have an expanded Start Menu, Startup and Resume is faster, more built in security, Apps are in Tabulated Form, Four (4) Apps in one place and all open task in a single view. The user can create Virtual Desktops when you need more space.

Microsoft EDGE allows the user to type Notes directly on Web pages and read "on line" articles and Save for later. A new IE Internet Explorer vers 12 or higher is provided. CORTANA, the new PDA , allow the user to make Reservations, read Reviews and has Voice Recognition.

A CLOSER LOOK AT BASIC COMPUTERS
(A simple explanation)

Computers are: Task driven machines, they can handle several tasks at the same time, which puts them in the category of " Multi-tasking ".

They speak their own Language, but understands many languages with the help of a " Translator ".
The Computer language is a binary language that represents zero (0) and (1) one., and is Digital.

The smallest unit of Information that can be Transmitted and/or Received in the Computer binary language, is called a BIT.

Because the BIT is very small, it is divided into groups of 8 BITS (01011101) and is called a BYTE. One BYTE is equal to 8 bits. (8 bits=1 BYTE).

BYTES are still too small, and are divided into a group of 8 BYTES in order to transmit and receive a WORD. (8 BYTES = 1 Word).

Because computers use their own language (binary) they need a Translator in order to transmit large amounts of WORDS called "DATA".

The METRIC system is used to organize the DATA. KILO is used to represent 1.000 (One thousand) MEGA is used to represent 1 Million

GIGA is used to represent 1 Billion and TERA is used to represent 1 Trillion.

When using these values they are:

One thousand Bytes is 1 Kb or One Kilobyte
One million Bytes is 1 Mb or One Million Bytes
One billion Bytes is 1 GB or One Billion Bytes
One trillion Bytes is 1 Tb or One Trillion Bytes

Computer Memory is called "RAM" Random Access Memory, and is divided into 1GB, 2GB, 4GB, 8GB, 16GB, 32GB, 64GB, 128GB etc.. Computers must follow this Standard. Some Computers are sold with 3GB and 6GB which is totally Unacceptable; and violates the Standards.

Computer Storage or built-in Hard Drive is divided into 250 GB, 500GB, 1 Tb, and 1.5 Tb. One Terabyte (1 Tb.) is recommended for Computer Internal Storage.

Computers are divided into HARDWARE and SOFTWARE, The Arithmetic Logic Unit (ALU) is a major Central Area of the Computer. It contains the CPU (Central Processing Unit) Memory, Storage, Network Cards, ROM (Read only Memory) and PROM (Programmable Memory); the Input and the Output.

The Input is the Keyboard, Mouse, Microphone, Tape /DVD/CD, Touch Pad, Video Input, Network Ports, Printer Port and Battery Port.

The Output Port is the Video Monitor, Speakers, Audio/Video Ports, HDMI Ports, USB Ports, Network Ports, Printer Port and Video Port.

The Central Processing Unit (CPU) is the Computer Heart. The speed of the Computer Processor CPU is measured in "cycles" or "Hertz) per second.
 1 Hertz (1 Hz.) = 1 cycle per second (cps.).

The minimum CPU Speed should be 2.5 Ghz (Gigahertz) A fast computer will have a Processor of 2.8 Ghz., 3.0 Ghz or higher.. Processors are Single core, Dual core or Quad core. Recommended INTEL Processors Dual Core i-5, i-7, i-8 or higher.

INTEL is the largest manufacturer of Processors in the World. Processors are also made by AMD and MOTOROLA and IBM. The INTEL Xeon Processors, Quad-Core i7, i-8, i-9 and beyond; are the fastest Processors (CPU) s' and are rated at 3.5 Ghz and beyond...

Computers are task driven machines, and are faster than humans in obtaining results and displaying it. Computers use " Analytical Thinking", and mathematical probabilities with multi-tasking.

 In general Humans use: Critical Thinking, Logical Thinking, Conditional Thinking, Analytical Thinking, Comparative Thinking, and Reasoning, part of our Natural Language development; all are used at the same time, to obtain results, which may take a longer or shorter time to display them. This makes us different from machines; in the way we process information. Computers can not think like humans.

Machines (computers) use Analytical thinking based on Tasks as requested by the User. Computers are Task driven machines. Sometimes we are looking for information in the wrong places, and assume that computers can and will go to the correct place to find the information for us.

We forget their limitations and did not give the machine a Clear Task to do. We assume that the Computer knows where to go to find the information; even tough, we did not give it the correct Task.; a "where" to go, and a "what" we are looking for.

Sometimes we need to think like machines, Analytical Thinking. To convey to the machine WHAT we want and WHERE we want to go., as an example. Our requests will always need to be "converted" to Zero's and One's. The Machine Language.

When we are looking for information on the INTERNET and we use a Computer with the necessary software and hardware requirements, we need to go to the correct places on the Internet, so that the Computer Software and System can work to find the information we are looking for.

CHAPTER THREE

FREE SOFTWARE and UTILITIES.

The Question becomes; WHERE do we go:

For Software Applications, and Utilities; we go to:

 FREEWARE, OPEN SOURCE, PUBLIC DOMAIN and TRIALWARE for 100% success.
What type of Internet Browser should be used ? The most popular Internet Browsers are: BING, YAHOO,

GOOGLE, FIREFOX, MSN, etc...

In asking the computer to SEARCH for specific things it is recommended that the Users get to know the basic SEARCH OPERATORS used on the INTERNET. The Plus (+) or Minus (-) and the Wild-card (*.*) or AND - OR-NAND-NOT, etc.. to help the computer find what we want. Example: SEARCH Cars NOT Vans., or SEARCH Truck's NOT Suv's.

A Natural Language Search Engine or a Semantic Search Engine for a more Organized, Complete and Tabulated response.
One of the best Semantic Search Engine on the Internet is: " DuckDuckGo ", Ask.com, Dogpile.Web and WebCrawler.

Machines and the Human Basic Information Process.

Computers as Task Driven Machines, contains the ALU with INPUT and OUTPUT, we know the INPUT is a Keyboard, Mouse, Tape, Microphone or other Input devices; and the OUTPUT is the Video Monitor, Tape Recorder,Video Display Device, Disk, Flash Drive, or other Output devices.

The ALU Arithmetic Logic Unit, also contains the OS or

Operating System, RAM Random Access Memory, ROM Read Only Memory, PROM Programmable Memory, the CPU Central Processing Unit, the heart of the Computer; also contains MOM and DAD.

MOM is Microsoft Operations Manager, with the built-in MMC Microsoft Management Console; a powerful Utility that enable the User to Manage his own Computer(s) and also gives the user the ability to create " SNAP-INS " to Secure, Manage and Setup the Computer, from a Console Root.

DAD Data Access Devices, that handles all Internal and external Monitoring functions within the ALU, and the Built-in Diagnostics.

All of these different areas are part of the Machine Process. This Process requires the machine(s) to use RULES, STANDARDS, PROTOCOLS, POLICIES, LAWS, and Analog and Digital Processing, and some machines can use Pure Mathematics, Empirical and Imaginary Numbers using SPI's and SPO's as part of the process.

SPI (Spy's) are Supervised Parallel Input's and SPO's are Supervised Parallel Outputs., to Monitor the Machine's Hardware and Software during the processing.

The Human Process.

Humans use Critical Thinking, Conditional Thinking,

Logical Thinking, Analytical Thinking, Comparative Thinking, and Multi Tasking as part of the process.
All of these Processes can occur at the same time, or in sequence.

The First Standards

To better understand Computers, it is very important to understand STANDARDS and how they work, and the First Standards used in Computers.

The Organization that regulates these Standards is ISO, the International Standards Organization.

The first Standards were developed aprox. In the 1960's and were implemented during the Video Displays and Printers development.

Some of first Video Standards were:

R-G-B Red Green Blue, developed by SONY Corp.,
C-M-Y-K(0-1) Cyan Magenta Yellow K Constant representing zero (0) or (1);
 PANTONE Certified Colors (PCC)

and CROMALIN developed by DUPONT, USA.
 Standards were then divided into three (3) Main Groups:
 Group 1) LOCAL, NATIONAL, INTERNATIONAL and DEFACTO.
 Group 2) Open Standards
 Group 3) Propitiatory Standards, IE. Sony.

Defacto Standards are HP-GPIB, PDL, PDF, USB 3.0 International Standards were Graphics Software, JPEG, TIFF, GIF, Sony VAIO Standards. Standards that were given for everyone or anyone to use were called "DEFACTO" Standards, and were FREE.

Propitiatory Standards are: ASAHI-PENTAX, SONY, HP, SAMSUNG, and CANON, to name just a few..

The International Standards organization then promoted three areas on the Internet for basic Software and Computer Information Systems open to both Business and Technology Research and Development:

1. FREEWARE
2. TRIALWARE
3. PUBLIC DOMAIN
4. OPEN SOURCE

Companies like Adobe, Hewlett Packard (HP), and others; began developing their own Standards:

- PDL Postscript Description Language
- PDF   Postscript Description Format (File)
- HPGL HP Graphics Language (used by printers)
- HPIB   HP Internal Buss
- GPIB   General Purpose Interface Buss

Internet Standards:

HTML   Hypertext Markup Language
XML   Extensible Markup Language

CHAPTER FOUR

A CLOSE LOOK AT SOFTWARE

Software are programs that run on the Computer, and are divided into three major parts;   APPLICATIONS, UTILITIES, and OPERATING SYSTEMS.

The   APPLICATIONS   Software   are   divided   into Multimedia Applications, WEB Applications, Security Applications, and USER Applications.

OPERATING   SYSTEMS   (OS) are Windows OS Software like Windows 8 or 10, LINUX, or other platforms Software OS., like Apple Macintosh OS, etc..

UTILITIES are small programs written to manage or protect the Computers. Utilities are made by many companies, such as NORTON UTILITIES, PANDA UTILITIES, ACEBYTE UTILITIES, etc..

Software is also divided into Special Areas on the Internet., such as: OPEN SOURCE, PUBLIC DOMAIN, TRIALWARE and FREEWARE.

SOFTWARE APPLICATIONS AND TYPES

This type of Software program contains Protocols and Rules that govern the use of the Software and its process. They tell the user what to do and how to use the Software correctly.

The basic rule for software applications are:
ENABLE, UNINSTALL, INSTALL, DELETE, REMOVE, PURGE, DISABLE, DISCONNECT, KILL PROCESS, STOP PROCESS, and COMMAND LINE.

MULTIMEDIA SOFTWARE

Windows Multimedia Applications are divided into: Printing Applications, Game Applications, Office Applications, Multimedia Applications, Drawing and Painting Applications, and Network Applications.

All of these Applications use the same type or similar multimedia tools. Multimedia Applications come with Windows Media Player II and CD/DVD Burner Software.

The Drawing and Printing Applications includes PAINT Software and supports Adobe Illustrator, Adobe Photoshop and Adobe Premier with Multimedia tools.

The Office Application Suite supports a variety of

Multimedia Tools. NotePad and WordPad are included in the Word Processing Application of the Suite.
Network Applications are supported with Multimedia Tools and Network Monitor and Port Scanner, are built in., with several other tools that support multimedia.

Multimedia Application Tools use the same Rules to:
1. Install Applications vs. Run Applications
2. Uninstall Applications vs. Delete Applications
3. Add vs. Remove Applications
4. Utility vs. Applications
5. User Install vs. System Install.

For example; you can not Disable a program that was not Enabled.

Software Types

They are several Types of Software. The most important types are:

6. Security
7. Test
8. Trialware
9. Productivity
10. Web
11. Enterprise
12. Public Domain

13. Open Source
14. Freeware
15. Development
16. Holographic

All of these Types of Software and Programs are subject to attack, a destructive types of Software designed to do harm to the machines.

These types of Software are: WORMS, VIRUSES, TROJAN, ROOTKITS, ADAWARE, MALWARE, etc..

VIRUSES and other DESTRUCTIVE SOFTWARE.

VIRUS is a Program that spreads by Replicating itself into other Programs.

WORM is a self contained Program, that is self Replicating like a Virus, but does not attach itself.

TROJAN is a Program that appears to be useful, but contains malware. Example; A Utility that may harm your computer.

HOAX-VIRUS Worse kind of Virus, sends hoax messages to users.

MALWARE Any Software Program designed to cause harm.

ROOT-KITS A form of TROJAN, monitors traffic to and from your computer, and alters system files.

SPYWARE Affects E-Mail monitors and control part of your computer, by decreasing computer performance.
Users my Run the PERF Monitor Utility built in Windows to check on computer performance.

SPAM a nuisance, not a threat, its unsolicited mail, and may affect your E-Mail.

ADAWARE   like SPYWARE, it affects computer Performance.

PROTOCOLS and THE INTERNET DOMAIN.

Protocols are rules and regulations that tell the computer how to behave and perform. Protocols can not be changed, modified or altered. They are considered special standards that govern the technology. The main Internet Protocol is an address that identifies the Computer on the Network., and is called an IP. Which consist of four (4) groups of numbers.

Protocols and the Internet Standards are regulated by

ICANN (Internet Corporation for Assigned Names and Numbers.) and other organizations such as W3C2 World Wide Consortium, IEEE, and others.

ICANN assign's all of the TOP Level Domains used in the INTERNET. The top level domains are: .COM,

.EDU, .BIZ, .INFO, .GOV, .NAME, .MIL, .PRO, .NET, .ORG, .AERO and .COOP.

A DNS Domain Name Server stores Domain Names and Translates Domain Names into IP Address.

To operate on the Internet, a computer must have a combination of two Protocols called TCP/IP or Transport Control Protocol/ Internet Protocol.

For example; The Domain Name: www.scsite.com
 will have an IP Address of: 198.80.146.30

An Internet Web Address and/or Web Page would be:
http://www.nmsu.edu/careers/index.html
(PROTOCOL) (DOMAIN NAME) (PATH) (WEB PAGE NAME)

The INTERNET was developed in 1960 and the WWW World Wide Web in 1990.

A WEB PAGE is a World Wide Collection of Electronic Documents.
A WEB BROWSER is an Application Software to access WEB PAGES.

CHAPTER FIVE

INTERNET PROTOCOL and THE WORLD WIDE WEB.

The INTERNET Service begins with the WWW. World Wide Web, which displays a WEB Site with WEB Pages.
The Internet Protocol and or WEB Address is entered into the URL (Universal Resource Locator).

The Hypertext Transport Protocol with the Internet Protocol determines the WEB ADDRESS.

http:// **www.msn.com/index.html**
(Protocol)　(Domain Name)　(Web Page Name)

IP Address: 198.80.146.30
A software Program with a Search Engine (Google) , (Bing), (Yahoo), etc..is used to display Web sites and Web Pages.

A Web Browser is required to view WEB PAGES.
Web Browsers such as Microsoft Internet Explorer (IE), or Fire Fox, etc..

IP ADDRESSES ON THE INTERNET

The Domain Web Address is Translated into an IP Address, on the Internet.

IP Address : 198.80.146.30

For Example: http://www.microsoft.com
                    (Domain Name)

IP Address: 207. 46 . 197   .113
              (Identifies the Network) (Identifies the Computer)

SEARCH ENGINES on the INTERNET

 Many search engines exist on the Internet, its important to know the difference between them. Natural Language Search Engines and Semantic Search Engines are the most important

The most popular Search Engines are: HotBot.com, Excite.com, AlltheWeb.com, Altavista.com, AskJeeves.com, Lycos.com, Looksmart.com, Webcrawler.com, Overture.com, and Infospace.com., and Google.
Search Engines can be a PORTAL or a BRIDGE.

GRAPHIC FORMATS USED ON THE INTERNET

The following Graphic Formats are used on the WEB.
   1. .PNG Portable Network Graphics

2. .TIFF Tagged Image File Format
3. .GIF   Graphic Interchange Format
4. .BMP   BitMap
5. .JPEG Joint Photographic Experts Group
6. .PCX   PC Paintbrush

These Graphic formats are used on Multimedia Web Pages that support Animation.

In order to display and play Multimedia Applications on the Internet, the user WEB Browser must be capable of supporting Multimedia.

If the Browser does not support Multimedia, then there are special applications called" PLUG-IN's that will extend the capability of the Browsers. By installing a PLUG-IN the User will be able to display and play Multimedia Elements.

FREE Plug-Ins are available on the Internet.
For Multimedia 3D Graphics get " SHOCKWAVE PLAYER" from macromedia.com.

For Music Video, get QUICKTIME from Apple.com, For Graphics Animation, get "FLASHPLAYER" from macromedia.com. For MP3 AUDIO / CD get" LIQUIDPLAYER" from liquidaudio.com, For LIVE Audio and Video, get "REAL ONE PLAYER" from

Real.com, For PDF Files supporting Multimedia, get " ACROBAT READER" from Adobe.com

SEARCH OPERATORS

Search with _____> AND or +   _> Red Cars and Red Vans or Green Apples + Red Apples.

Search with __> OR ____> Flight Attendant OR Stewardess.

Search with ___> AND NOT (-) __> SUV AND NOT Auto, SUV – AUTO

Search with __> Phrase searching" Harry Potter" __> exact phrase within " quotation".

Search with " WILDCARD" __> Writ* or Clou* __The ASTERISK (*) at the end of words.

WINDOWS BUILT IN UTILITIES AND TOOLS TO KEEP THE COMPUTER CLEAN.

The following Utilities are built into Windows and can be access by the User for Troubleshooting, Monitoring and Maintenance of the Computer.

1. On-Screen Keyboard
2. Phone Companion
3. Phone
4. System Information
5. Uninstall Utility
6. Windows Memory Diagnostics
7. WinPatrol Explorer
8. WinPatrol Help
9. CMD Command Line.

The following Utilities can be downloaded Free from the Internet to Clean and keep the User Computer clean and free from Viruses and Harmful Software:

1. Advanced System Care 10.3
2. Glary Utilities
3. Acebyte Utilities
4. Clean Master
5. Malicious Removal Tool

The following Applications are built-into Windows and are available to the User for Maintenance and Troubleshooting of the Computer.

1. 3D Builder
2. Narrator
3. Performance Monitor
4. Resource Monitor
5. RUN
6. System Configuration
7. Task Manager

CHAPTER SIX

KEEPING THE COMPUTER CLEAN

Computers running Windows OS need to be cleaned periodically to keep the computer performance healthy and free from harmful programs like Viruses and Malware.

The following cleaners are required:

1. SYSTEM CLEANERS
2. REGISTRY CLEANERS
3. VIRUS CLEANERS
4. ADAWARE CLEANERS
5. SPYWARE CLEANERS
6. MALICIOUS REMOVAL TOOL

USER SETUP OF WINDOWS SECURITY

Built in Tools are available to the User to Setup the Security on the Windows Computer.

Windows Security Setup Tools are:
1. SECPOL.EXE
2. GPEDIT.EXE
3. SECURITY CONFIGURATION
4. WINDOWS FIREWALL
5. WINDOWS DEFENDER
6. MMC MICROSOFT MANAGEMENT CONSOLE.
7. SNAP-INS

COMPUTER APPLICATION AND UTILITIES

To find Free Application Software and Utilities for any Computer, the User can go to the following Areas on the Internet:

- PUBLIC DOMAIN
- OPEN SOURCE
- FREEWARE
- TRIALWARE
-

System Cleaners and Registry Cleaners and Utilities are

found at these locations. All Software are FREE to download and use.

A CLOSER LOOK AT WINDOWS 10 PRO

Windows 10 Professional comes with USB 3.0 Ports, built-in Technology for Holographic Software, a new Web Browser "EDGE", a new READ command that allows 'Read on Line" Articles and Save for later.

Type Notes directly on WEB Pages, a new Personal digital Assistant " CORTANA" , that can make

Reservations, Read Reviews, and support Voice Recognition, when spoken to.

A new Internet Explorer Vers. II
An expanded Start Menu, Startup and resume fast .

More built in Security, with Apps in Tabulated form four Apps in one place, all open Task in a single view.

Can create Virtual desktops when you need more space.

WINDOWS ULTIMATE TOOL FOR USER MAINTENANCE AND TROUBLESHOOTING.

This special Advanced folder contains more than 250 Files and Graphics to Maintain and Troubleshoot any and every part of the Computer.

This folder is created by the User from hidden Codes built into Windows.

To create the **Advanced Folder,**

1. Create a New folder on the desktop, and call it:
2. Advanced.
3. Put a period after the d.
4. Enter the **CODE** below after you Open Bracket, Close Bracket at the end.

OPEN BRACKET {
CLOSE BRACKET }

ADVANCED.{ED7BA470-8E54-465E-825C-99712043E01C} <ENTER>

The new green Folder is created containing 237 Files with graphics showing the User WHERE, WHEN and WHY to fix and troubleshoot the Computer.

WINDOWS BUILT IN (**MMC**) MICROSOFT
MANAGEMENT CONSOLE.

On the Startup or RUN Command, type: MMC

The Microsoft Management Console window will be
displayed.
Create "SNAP-IN's " from the Console Root Window
to Manager the Computer.

A step by step Guide is included to do this.

CHAPTER 7

Step-by-Step Guide to the Microsoft Management Console MMC.

The Microsoft Management Console (MMC) lets
system administrators create much more flexible
user interfaces and customize administration tools.
This step-by-step guide explores some of these new

features.

Introduction

MMC unifies and simplifies day-to-day system management tasks. It hosts tools and displays them as consoles. These tools, consisting of one or more applications, are **built with modules called snap-ins.** The snap-ins also can include additional extension snap-ins. MMC is a core part of Microsoft's management strategy and is included in Microsoft Windows operating systems. In addition, Microsoft development groups will use MMC for future management applications.

Microsoft Management Console enables system administrators to create special tools to delegate specific administrative tasks to users or groups. Microsoft provides standard tools with the operating system that perform everyday administrative tasks that users need to accomplish. These are part of the **All Users** profile of the computer and located in the **Administrative Tools** group on the **Startup** menu. Saved as MMC console (.msc) files, these custom tools can be sent by e-mail, shared in a network folder, or posted on the Web. They can also be assigned to users, groups, or computers with system policy settings. A tool can be scaled up and down, integrated seamlessly into the operating system, repackaged, and customized.

Using MMC, system administrators can create unique consoles for workers who report to them or for workgroup managers. They can assign a tool with a system policy, deliver the file by e-mail, or post the file to a shared location on the network. When a workgroup manager opens the .msc file, access will be restricted to those tools provided by the system administrator.

Building your own tools with the standard user interface in MMC is a straightforward process. Start with an existing console and modify or add components to fulfill your needs. Or create an entirely new console. The following example shows how to create a new console and arrange its administrative components into separate windows.

Prerequisites and Requirements

There are no prerequisites: you don't need to complete any other step-by-step guide before starting this guide. You need one computer running either Windows Professional or Windows. For the most current information about hardware requirements and compatibility for servers, clients, and peripherals, see the Check Hardware and Software Compatibility page on the Windows website.

Creating Consoles

The most common way for administrators to use MMC is to simply start a predefined console file from the Start menu. However, to get an idea of the flexibility of MMC, it is useful to create a console file from scratch. It is also useful to create a console file from scratch when using the new task delegation features in this version of MMC.

Creating a New Console File

- On the Start Menu, click **Run**, type **MMC**, and then click **OK**. Microsoft Management Console opens with an empty console (or administrative tool) as shown in Figure 1 below. The empty console has no management functionality until you add some snap-ins. The MMC menu commands on the menu bar at the top of the Microsoft Management Console window apply to the entire console.

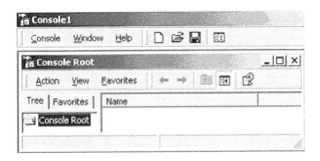

Figure 1: Beginning Console Window

- Click Console (under Console1). On the Console Menu, click **Add/Remove Snap-in**. The Add/Remove Snap-in dialog box opens. This lets you enable extensions and configure which snap-ins are in the console file. You can specify where the snap-ins should be inserted in the **Snap-in's "added to** drop-down box." Accept the default, **Console Root**, for this exercise.

- Click **Add**. This displays the Add Standalone Snap-in dialog box that lists the snap-ins that are installed on your computer.

- From the list of snap-ins, double-click **Computer Management** to open the **Computer Management** wizard.

- Click **Local computer** and select the check box for "**Allow the selected computer to be changed**

when launching from the command line."

- Click **Finish**. This returns you to the **Add/Remove Snap-ins** dialog box. Click **Close**.

- Click the **Extensions** tab as shown in Figure 2 below. By selecting the check box **Add all extensions**, all locally-installed extensions on the computer are used. If this check box is not selected, then any extension snap-in that is selected is explicitly loaded when the console file is opened on a different computer.

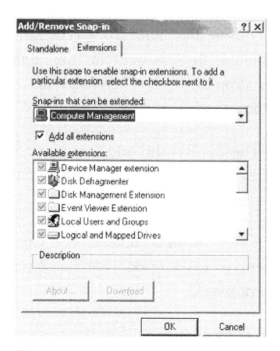

Figure 2: Select All Extensions

- Click **OK** to close the Add/Remove Snap-in dialog box. The Console Root window now has a snap-in, **Computer Management**, rooted at the Console Root folder.

Customizing the Display of Snap-ins in the Console: New Windows

After you add the snap-ins, you can add windows to provide different administrative views in the console.

To add windows

- In the left pane of the tree view in Figure 3 below, click the **+** next to **Computer Management**. Click **System Tools**.

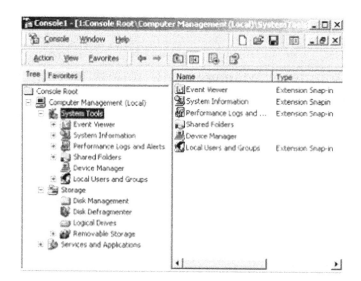

Figure 3: Console1: System Tools

- Right-click the **Event Viewer** folder that opens, and then click **New window** from here. As shown in Figure 4 below, this opens a new Event Viewer window rooted at the Event Viewer extension to computer management.

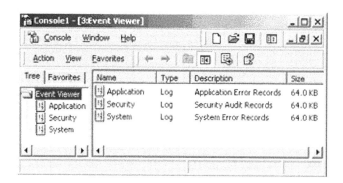

Figure 4: Event Viewer

- Click **Window** and click **Console Root**.

- In the Console Root window, click **Services and Applications**, right-click **Services** in the left pane, and then click **New Window**. As shown in Figure 5 below, this opens a new Services window rooted at the Event Viewer extension to Computer Management. In the new window, click the **Show/Hide Console Tree** toolbar button to hide the console tree, as shown in the red circle in Figure 5 below.

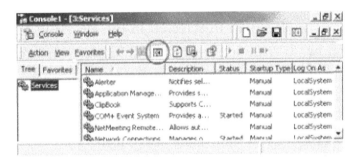

Figure 5: Show/Hide Button

- Close the original window with Console Root showing in it.

- On the Window menu, select **Tile Horizontally**. The console file should appear and include the information shown in Figure 4 and Figure 5 above.

- You can now save your new MMC console. Click the **Save as** icon on the Console window, and give your console a name. Your console is now saved as a .msc file, and you can provide it to anyone who needs to configure a computer with these tools.

Note: Each of the two smaller windows has a toolbar with buttons and drop-down menus. The toolbar buttons and drop-down menus on these each of these two windows apply only to the contents of the window. You can see that a window's toolbar buttons and menus change depending on the snap-in selected in the left pane of the window. If you select the View menu, you can see a list of available toolbars.

Tip: The windows fit better if your monitor display is set to a higher resolution and small font.

Creating Console Taskpads

If you are creating a console file for another user, it's useful to provide a very simplified view with only a few tasks available. Console taskpads help you to do this.

To create a console taskpad

13. From the Window menu, select **New Window**. Close the other two windows (you will save a new console file at the end of this procedure). Maximize the remaining window.

14. In the left pane, click the **+** next to the **Computer Management** folder, then click the **+** next to the **System Tools** folder. Click **System**, click the **Event Viewer** folder, right-click **System**, and select **New Taskpad** View.

15. Go through the wizard accepting all the default settings. Verify the checkbox on the last page is checked so that the Task Creation wizard can start automatically.

16. Choose the defaults in the Task Creation wizard until you come to the page shown below in Figure 6, then choose a list view task and select **Properties**:

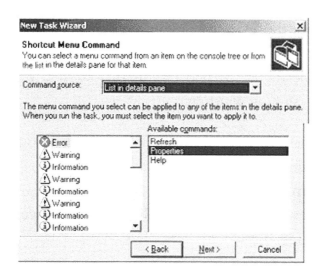

Figure 6: New Task Wizard

17. Click **Next** and accept the defaults for the rest of the screens. By selecting an Event and clicking **Properties**, you can see the property page for that Event.

   After you click **Finish** on the last screen, your console should look like Figure 7 below:

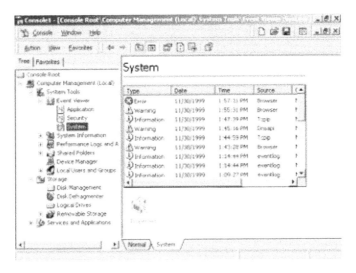

Figure 7: New Console Showing System Event Log

18. Click the **Show/Hide console tree** toolbar button.

19. From the view menu, click **Customize** and click each of the options except the Description bar to hide each type of toolbar.

The next section discusses how to lock the console file down so that the user sees only a limited view. For right now your console file should look like Figure 8 below.

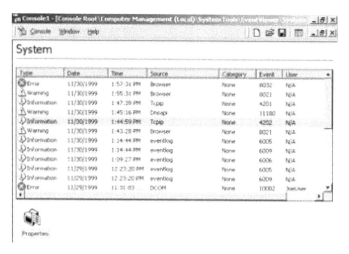

Figure 8: Customized View

Setting Console File Options

If you are creating a console file for another user, it is useful to prevent that user from further customizing the console file. The Options dialog box allows you to do this.

To set console file options

5. From the **Console** menu, select **Options**.

6. Change the Console Mode by selecting **User Modelimited access, single window** from the drop-down dialog box. This will prevent a user from adding new snap-ins to the console file or

rearranging the windows.

7. You can change the name from Console1. Click **OK** to continue.

8. **Save** the console file. The changes will not take effect until the console file is opened again.

This is just one example of how the Microsoft Management Console lets you group information and functionality that previously would have required opening a Control Panel option plus two separate administrative tools. The modular architecture of MMC makes it easy for system network developers to create snap-in applications that leverage the platform while easing administrative load.

CHAPTER 8

HIDDEN APPLICATIONS and UTILITIES

 Windows contain many hidden Applications and Utilities available to the User, that can be used to manage and troubleshoot the computer.

1.   The special ADVANCE Folder

2.   EXPLORER SHELL

3.   The " ALL APPLICATIONS FOLDER"

All of these are created by the User by entering the hidden Codes. The special ADVANCED folder is covered elsewhere in this book, we will look at EXPLORER SHELL.

Create a portable folder of any part of Windows system, IE, Control Panel, Documents, Drives, etc.. using Explorer Shell.

1. Create a short cut Folder by selecting NEW and then Shortcut on your Desktop.

2. In the shortcut window type: Explorer Shell: and the name of the part of Windows you want to create:

for example;

Explorer Shell: ControlPanelFolder   and click NEXT, another window will be displayed.

3. Type the name you want to give to the Folder, and press FINISH, the new Folder will be created.

The Folder created will be portable, and can be used on any Windows Computer. All of the Control Panels will be available in the Folder, by just one click. Saving three steps in Windows, to get to the Control Panels.

4. The following is a list of All the locations in Windows that can be created.

5. List:

WINDOWS SHELL COMMANDS.___

Shell Command	Description
shell:AccountPictures	Account Pictures
shell:AddNewProgramsFolder	The "Get Programs" Control panel item

shell:Administrative Tools   Administrative Tools

shell:AppData   Same as %appdata%, the c:\user\<username>\appdata\roaming folder

shell:Application Shortcuts   Opens the folder which stores all Modern apps shortcuts

shell:AppsFolder   The virtual folder which stores all installed Modern apps

shell:AppUpdatesFolder   The "Installed Updates" Control panel item

shell:Cache   IE's cache folder (Temporary Internet Files)

shell:CD Burning   Temporary Burn Folder

shell:ChangeRemoveProgramsFolder   The "Uninstall a program" Control panel item shell:Common Administrative Tools   The Administrative Tools folder for all users

shell:Common   AppData   The C:\ProgramData folder (%ProgramData%)

shell:Common Desktop   Public Desktop

shell:Common   Documents   Public Documents

shell:Common   Programs   All Users Programs, which are part of Start menu. Still used by the Start screen

shell:Common   Start   Menu   All Users Start Menu folder, same as above

shell:Common   Startup   The   Startup folder, used for all users

shell:Common   Templates   Same   as above,   but   used   for   new   documents templates, e.g. by Microsoft

Office

shell:CommonDownloads	Public Downloads
shell:CommonMusic	Public Music
shell:CommonPictures	Public Pictures
shell:CommonRingtones	Public Ringtones folder
shell:CommonVideo	Public Videos
shell:ConflictFolder	The Control Panel\All Control Panel Items\Sync Center\Conflicts item
shell:ConnectionsFolder	The Control Panel\All Control Panel Items\Network Connections item
shell:Contacts	Contacts folder (Address book)
shell:ControlPanelFolder	**Control Panel**

shell:Cookies	The folder with IE's cookies

shell:CredentialManager
C:\Users\<username>\AppData\Roaming\Microsoft\Credentials

shell:CryptoKeys
C:\Users\<username>\AppData\Roaming\Microsoft\Crypto

shell:CSCFolder	This folder is broken in Windows 8/7, provides access to the Offline files item

shell:Desktop	Desktop

shell:Device Metadata Store
C:\ProgramData\Microsoft\Windows\DeviceMetadataStore

shell:DocumentsLibrary	Documents Library

shell:Downloads   **Downloads folder**

shell:DpapiKeys
C:\Users\<username>\AppData\Roaming\Micr
osoft\Protect

shell:Favorites   Favorites

shell:Fonts   C:\Windows\Fonts

shell:Games   The Games Explorer
item

shell:GameTasks

shell:HomeGroupFolder   The Home Group root folder

shell:ImplicitAppShoC:\Users\<username>\AppData
\Local\Microsoft\Windows\GameExplorer

shell:History
C:\Users\<username>\AppData\Local\Microsoft
\Windows\History, IE's browsing history

shell:HomeGroupCurrentUserFolder   The
Home Group folder for the current user

rtcuts

C:\Users\<username>\AppData\Roaming\Micr osoft\Internet Explorer\Quick Launch\User Pinned\ImplicitAppShortcuts

shell:InternetFolder **This** **shell command will start Internet Explorer**

shell:Libraries   Libraries

shell:Links   The "Favorites" folder from the Explorer navigation pane.

shell:Local   AppData C:\Users\<username>\AppData\Local

shell:LocalAppDataLow C:\Users\<username>\AppData\LocalLow

shell:LocalizedResourcesDir   This   shell folder is broken in Windows 8

shell:MAPIFolder   Represents the Microsoft Outlook folder

shell:MusicLibrary   **Music Library**

shell:My Music   The "My Music" folder (not the Library)

shell:My Pictures   The "My Pictures" folder (not the Library)

shell:My Video   The "My Videos" folder (not the Library)

shell:MyComputerFolder
Computer/Drives view

shell:NetHood
C:\Users\<username>\AppData\Roaming\Micr osoft\Windows\Network Shortcuts

shell:NetworkPlacesFolder   The Network Places folder which shows computers and devices on your network

shell:OEM Links   This shell command does nothing on my Windows 8 Retail edition. Maybe it works with OEM Windows 8 editions.

shell:Original Images   Not functional on

Windows 8

shell:Personal The "My Documents" folder (not the Library)

shell:PhotoAlbums Saved slideshows, seems to have not been implemented yet

shell:PicturesLibrary Pictures Library

shell:Playlists Stores WMP Playlists.

shell:PrintersFolder The classic "Printers" folder (not 'Devices and Printers')

shell:PrintHood C:\Users\<username>\AppData\Roaming\Microsoft\Windows\Printer Shortcuts

shell:Profile The User profile folder

shell:ProgramFiles **Program Files**

shell:ProgramFilesCommon C:\Program Files\Common Files

shell:ProgramFilesCommonX86
C:\Program Files (x86)\Common Files - for Windows x64

shell:ProgramFilesX86 C:\Program Files (x86) - for Windows x64

shell:Programs
C:\Users\<username>\AppData\Roaming\Microsoft\Windows\Start Menu\Programs (Per-user Start Menu Programs folder)

shell:Public C:\Users\Public

shell:PublicAccountPictures
C:\Users\Public\AccountPictures

shell:PublicGameTasks
C:\ProgramData\Microsoft\Windows\GameExplorer

shell:PublicLibraries
C:\Users\Public\Libraries

shell:Quick Launch

C:\Users\<username>\AppData\Roaming\Micr osoft\Internet Explorer\Quick Launch

shell:Recent   The "Recent Items" folder (Recent Documents)

shell:RecordedTVLibrary   The "Recorded TV" Library

shell:RecycleBinFolder   Recycle Bin

shell:ResourceDir
 C:\Windows\Resources where visual styles are stored

shell:Ringtones
C:\Users\<username>\AppData\Local\Microso ft\Windows\Ringtones

shell:Roamed   Tile   Images   Is   not implemented yet. Reserved for future.

shell:Roaming   Tiles
     C:\Users\<username>\AppData\Local\Mi crosoft\Windows\RoamingTiles

shell:SavedGames   Saved Games

shell:Screenshots   The folder for Win+Print Screen screenshots

shell:Searches   Saved Searches

shell:SearchHomeFolder   Windows Search UI

shell:SendTo   The folder with items that you can see in the "Send to" menu

shell:Start   Menu
    C:\Users\<username>\AppData\Roaming\Microsoft\Windows\Start Menu (Per-user Start Menu folder)

shell:Startup   Per-user Startup folder

shell:SyncCenterFolder   Control Panel\All Control Panel Items\Sync Center

shell:SyncResultsFolder   Control Panel\All

Control Panel Items\Sync Center\Sync Results

shell:SyncSetupFolder   Control Panel\All Control Panel Items\Sync Center\Sync Setup

shell:System
C:\Windows\System32

shell:SystemCertificates
C:\Users\<username>\AppData\Roaming\Micr osoft\SystemCertificates

shell:SystemX86
C:\Windows\SysWOW64 -Windows x64 only

shell:Templates
C:\Users\<username>\AppData\Roaming\Micr osoft\Windows\Templates

Templates

shell:User Pinned   Pinned items for Taskbar and Start screen, C:\Users\<username>\AppData\Roaming\Micr osoft\Internet Explorer\Quick Launch\User Pinned

shell:UserProfiles   C:\Users, the users folder where the user profiles are stored

shell:UserProgramFiles   Not implemented yet. Reserved for future.

shell:UserProgramFilesCommon   same as above

shell:UsersFilesFolder   The current user profile

shell:UsersLibrariesFolder   Libraries

shell:VideosLibrary   Videos Library

shell:Windows   C:\Windows

shell:DpapiKeys C:\Users\<username>\AppData\Roaming\Microsoft\Protect

shell:Favorites	Favorites
shell:Fonts	**C:\Windows\Fonts**
shell:Games	The Games Explorer item
shell:GameTasks	C:\Users\<username>\AppData\Local\Microsoft\Windows\GameExplorer
shell:History	C:\Users\<username>\AppData\Local\Microsoft\Windows\History, IE's browsing history
shell:HomeGroupCurrentUserFolder	The Home Group folder for the current user
shell:HomeGroupFolder	The Home Group root folder
shell:ImplicitAppShortcuts	C:\Users\<username>\AppData\Roaming\Microsoft\Internet Explorer\Quick Launch\User Pinned\ImplicitAppShortcuts

shell:InternetFolder   This   shell
command will start Internet Explorer

shell:Libraries   Libraries

shell:Links   The "Favorites" folder
from the Explorer navigation pane.

shell:Local   AppData
C:\Users\<username>\AppData\Local

shell:LocalAppDataLow
C:\Users\<username>\AppData\LocalLow

shell:LocalizedResourcesDir   This   shell
folder is broken in Windows 8

shell:MAPIFolder   Represents   the
Microsoft Outlook folder

shell:MusicLibrary   Music Library

shell:My Music   The "My Music"
folder (not the Library)

shell:My Pictures   The "My Pictures"

folder (not the Library)

shell:My Video   The "My Videos" folder (not the Library)

shell:MyComputerFolder Computer/Drives view

shell:NetHood C:\Users\<username>\AppData\Roaming\Micr osoft\Windows\Network Shortcuts

shell:NetworkPlacesFolder The Network Places folder which shows computers and devices on your network

shell:OEM Links   This shell command does nothing on my Windows 8 Retail edition. Maybe it works with OEM Windows 8 editions.

shell:Original Images   Not functional on Windows 8

shell:Personal   The "My Documents" folder (not the Library)

shell:PhotoAlbums   Saved slideshows, seems to have not been implemented yet

shell:PicturesLibrary   Pictures Library

shell:Playlists   Stores WMP Playlists.

shell:PrintersFolder   The classic "Printers" folder (not 'Devices and Printers')

shell:PrintHood
C:\Users\<username>\AppData\Roaming\Microsoft\Windows\Printer Shortcuts

shell:Profile   The User profile folder

shell:ProgramFiles   Program Files

shell:Programs
C:\Users\<username>\AppData\Roaming\Microsoft\Windows\Start Menu\Programs (Per-user Start Menu Programs folder)

shell:Public   C:\Users\Public

shell:PublicAccountPictures

C:\Users\Public\AccountPictures

shell:PublicGameTasks
C:\ProgramData\Microsoft\Windows\GameExplorer

shell:PublicLibraries
C:\Users\Public\Libraries

shell:Quick Launch
C:\Users\<username>\AppData\Roaming\Microsoft\Internet Explorer\Quick Launch

shell:Recent The "Recent Items" folder (Recent Documents)

shell:RecordedTVLibrary The "Recorded TV" Library

shell:RecycleBinFolder Recycle Bin

shell:ResourceDir
C:\Windows\Resources where visual styles are stored

shell:Ringtones
C:\Users\<username>\AppData\Local\Microso
ft\Windows\Ringtones

shell:Roamed Tile Images   Is not
implemented yet. Reserved for future.

shell:Roaming   Tiles
C:\Users\<username>\AppData\Local\Microso
ft\Windows\RoamingTiles

shell:SavedGames   Saved Games

shell:Screenshots   The folder for
Win+Print Screen screenshots

shell:Searches   Saved Searches

shell:SearchHomeFolder   Windows Search
UI

shell:SendTo   The folder with
items that you can see in the "Send to" menu

shell:Start   Menu

C:\Users\<username>\AppData\Roaming\Micr osoft\Windows\Start Menu (Per-user Start Menu folder)

shell:Startup   Per-user   Startup folder

shell:SyncCenterFolder   Control Panel\All Control Panel Items\Sync Center

shell:SyncResultsFolder   Control Panel\All Control Panel Items\Sync Center\Sync Results

shell:SyncSetupFolder   Control Panel\All   Control   Panel   Items\Sync Center\Sync Setup

shell:System
C:\Windows\System32

shell:SystemCertificates
C:\Users\<username>\AppData\Roaming\Micr osoft\SystemCertificates

shell:SystemX86

C:\Windows\SysWOW64 -Windows x64 only

shell:Templates
C:\Users\<username>\AppData\Roaming\Micr
osoft\Windows\Templates

shell:User Pinned   Pinned items for
Taskbar   and   Start   screen,
C:\Users\<username>\AppData\Roaming\Micr
osoft\Internet Explorer\Quick Launch\User
Pinned

shell:UserProfiles   C:\Users, the users
folder where the user profiles are stored

shell:UserProgramFiles   Not
implemented yet. Reserved for future.

shell:UserProgramFilesCommon   same as
above

shell:UsersFilesFolder   The current user
profile

shell:UsersLibrariesFolder   Libraries

shell:VideosLibrary	Videos Library
shell:Windows	C:\Windows

CHAPTER 9

To create the " All Applications Folder", which will contain all of the "Hidden" Applications and Utilities and make them visible and accessible to the user; then all the hidden files and folder will be available.

1. Create a Blank folder on the desktop, and call it Applications. Put a period. At the end of s.

2. Open Bracket { and type in the **CODE**, then Close Bracket }

3. Press <ENTER>

4. **CODE**

Applications.{4234d49b-0245-4df3-

b780-3893943456e1} The Folder will be created.

GRAPHICS OF THIS BOOK.

These Graphics were created from the Text in this Book. For more information on how these were created, contact the Author at amazon.com

COMPUTER VIRUSSES. —

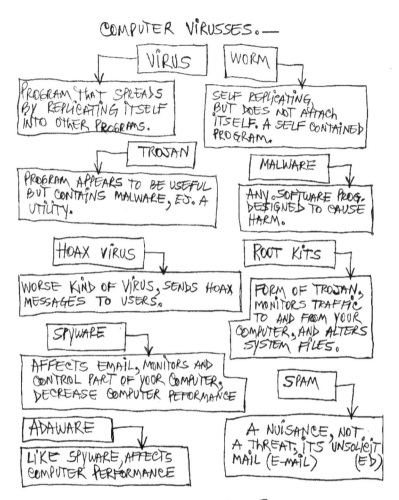

VIRUS

PROGRAM THAT SPREADS BY REPLICATING ITSELF INTO OTHER PROGRAMS.

WORM

SELF REPLICATING, BUT DOES NOT ATTACH ITSELF. A SELF CONTAINED PROGRAM.

TROJAN

PROGRAM APPEARS TO BE USEFUL BUT CONTAINS MALWARE, EJ. A UTILITY.

MALWARE

ANY SOFTWARE PROG. DESIGNED TO CAUSE HARM.

HOAX VIRUS

WORSE KIND OF VIRUS, SENDS HOAX MESSAGES TO USERS.

ROOT KITS

FORM OF TROJAN, MONITORS TRAFFIC TO AND FROM YOUR COMPUTER, AND ALTERS SYSTEM FILES.

SPYWARE

AFFECTS EMAIL, MONITORS AND CONTROL PART OF YOUR COMPUTER, DECREASE COMPUTER PETFORMANCE

SPAM

ADAWARE

LIKE SPYWARE, AFFECTS COMPUTER PERFORMANCE

A NUISANCE, NOT A THREAT, ITS UNSOLICIT MAIL (E-MAIL) (ED)

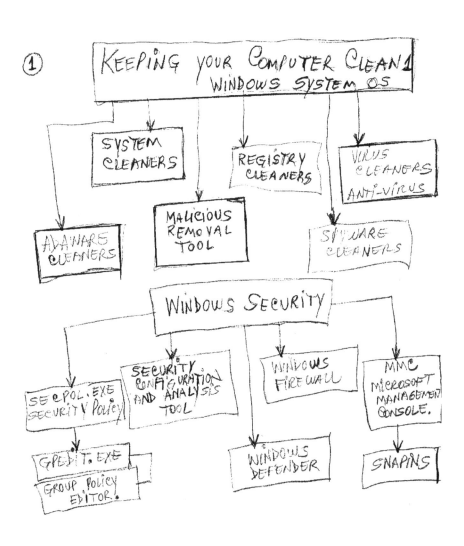

① KEEPING YOUR COMPUTER CLEAN 1
WINDOWS SYSTEM OS

SYSTEM CLEANERS

REGISTRY CLEANERS

VIRUS CLEANERS
ANTI-VIRUS

ADWARE CLEANERS

MALICIOUS REMOVAL TOOL

SPYWARE CLEANERS

WINDOWS SECURITY

SECPOL.EXE SECURITY POLICY

SECURITY CONFIGURATION AND ANALYSIS TOOL

WINDOWS FIREWALL

MMC MICROSOFT MANAGEMENT CONSOLE.

GPEDIT.EXE GROUP POLICY EDITOR.

WINDOWS DEFENDER

SNAPINS

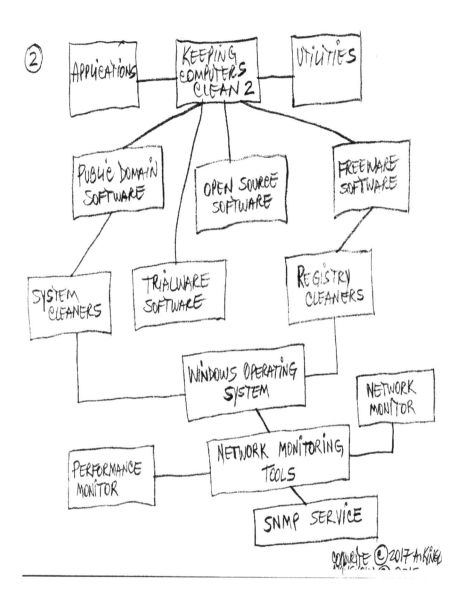

② Applications — Keeping Computers Clean 2 — Utilities

Public Domain Software

Open Source Software

Freeware Software

System Cleaners

Trialware Software

Registry Cleaners

Windows Operating System

Network Monitor

Performance Monitor

Network Monitoring Tools

SNMP Service

MACHINE AND HUMAN BASIC INFORMATION PROCESS.—

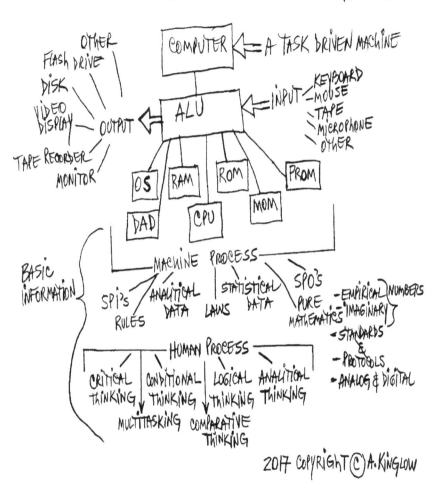

2017 COPYRIGHT Ⓒ A. KINGLOW

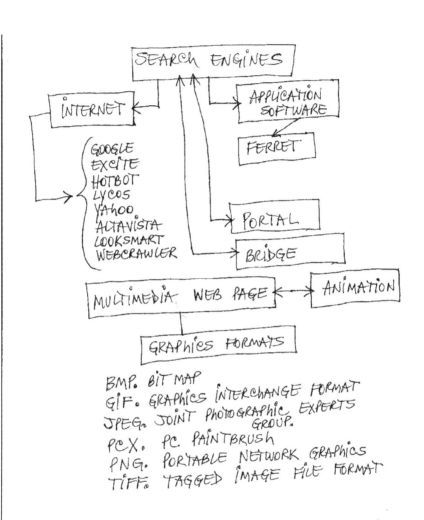

SEARCH ENGINES

INTERNET

APPLICATION SOFTWARE

FERRET

GOOGLE
EXCITE
HOTBOT
LYCOS
YAHOO
ALTAVISTA
LOOKSMART
WEBCRAWLER

PORTAL

BRIDGE

MULTIMEDIA WEB PAGE

ANIMATION

GRAPHICS FORMATS

BMP. BIT MAP
GIF. GRAPHICS INTERCHANGE FORMAT
JPEG. JOINT PHOTOGRAPHIC EXPERTS GROUP.
PCX. PC PAINTBRUSH
PNG. PORTABLE NETWORK GRAPHICS
TIFF. TAGGED IMAGE FILE FORMAT

INTERNET SEARCH OPERATORS.
AND ENGINES FORMAT.—

| SEARCH WITH | → | AND OR (+) | → | RED CARS AND RED VANS. GREEN APPLES + RED APPLES. |

| SEARCH WITH | → | OR | → | (ONE WORD TO BE IN SEARCH.) FLIGHT ATTENDANT OR STEWARDESS. |

| SEARCH WITH | → | AND NOT (—) | → | SUV AND NOT AUTO SUV — AUTO |

| SEARCH WITH | → | PHRASE SEARCHING "HARRY POTTER" | → | EXACT PHRASE WITHIN QUOTATION |

| SEARCH WITH WILDCARD. | → | WRIT* CLOU* | → | THE ASTERISK (*) AT THE END OF WORDS. |

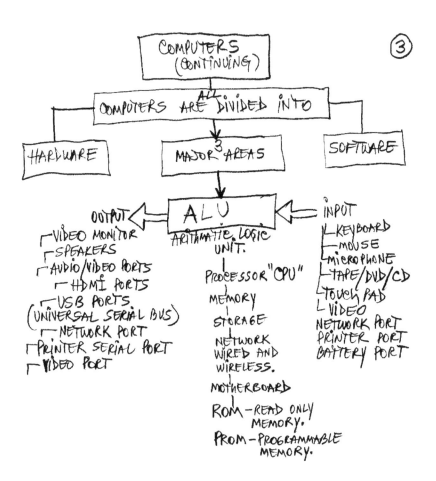

COMPUTERS
(CONTINUING)

③

COMPUTERS ARE ALL DIVIDED INTO

HARDWARE

3
MAJOR AREAS

SOFTWARE

OUTPUT ← ALU → INPUT

ARITHMATIC, LOGIC UNIT.

OUTPUT
- VIDEO MONITOR
- SPEAKERS
- AUDIO/VIDEO PORTS
- HDMI PORTS
- USB PORTS
(UNIVERSAL SERIAL BUS)
- NETWORK PORT
- PRINTER SERIAL PORT
- VIDEO PORT

PROCESSOR "CPU"

MEMORY
|
STORAGE

NETWORK
WIRED AND
WIRELESS.

MOTHERBOARD

ROM — READ ONLY
        MEMORY.

PROM — PROGRAMMABLE
         MEMORY.

INPUT
- KEYBOARD
- MOUSE
- MICROPHONE
- TAPE/DVD/CD
- TOUCH PAD
- VIDEO
NETWORK PORT
PRINTER PORT
BATTERY PORT

MACHINE AND HUMAN BASIC INFORMATION PROCESS.—

COMPUTER ⇐= A TASK DRIVEN MACHINE

OTHER
FLASH DRIVE
DISK
VIDEO DISPLAY
TAPE RECORDER
MONITOR

OUTPUT ⇐ ALU ⇐ INPUT

KEYBOARD
MOUSE
TAPE
MICROPHONE
OTHER

OS   RAM   ROM   PROM

DAD   CPU   MOM

BASIC INFORMATION

MACHINE PROCESS

SPI's   ANALITICAL DATA   STATISTICAL DATA   SPO's
RULES   LAWS   PURE MATHEMATICS

EMPIRICAL — NUMBERS
IMAGINARY
STANDARDS &
PROTOCOLS
ANALOG & DIGITAL

HUMAN PROCESS

CRITICAL THINKING   CONDITIONAL THINKING   LOGICAL THINKING   ANALITICAL THINKING

MULTITASKING   COMPARATIVE THINKING

2017 COPYRIGHT Ⓒ A. KINGLOW

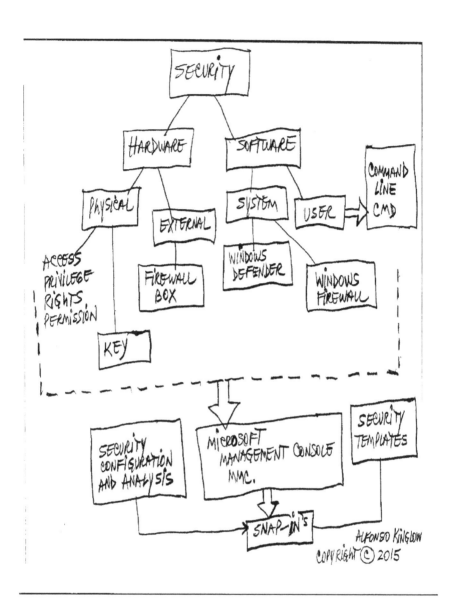

SECURITY

HARDWARE

SOFTWARE

COMMAND LINE CMD

PHYSICAL

EXTERNAL

SYSTEM

USER

ACCESS PRIVILEGE RIGHTS PERMISSION

FIREWALL BOX

WINDOWS DEFENDER

WINDOWS FIREWALL

KEY

SECURITY CONFIGURATION AND ANALYSIS

MICROSOFT MANAGEMENT CONSOLE MMC.

SECURITY TEMPLATES

SNAP-IN's

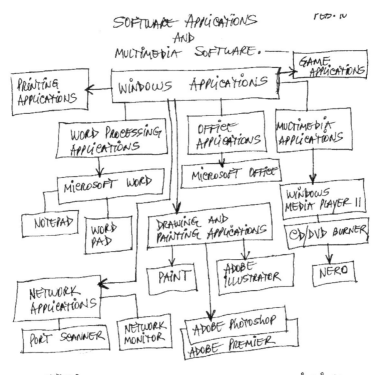

SOFTWARE APPLICATIONS AND MULTIMEDIA SOFTWARE. — FIG. IV

NOTE:

INSTALL APPLICATIONS VS. RUN APPLICATIONS
UNINSTALL APPLICATIONS VS. DELETE APPLICATIONS
ADD AND REMOVE APPLICATIONS (SOFTWARE)
UTILITY VS. APPLICATIONS
USER INSTALL VS. SYSTEM INSTALL APPLICATIONS

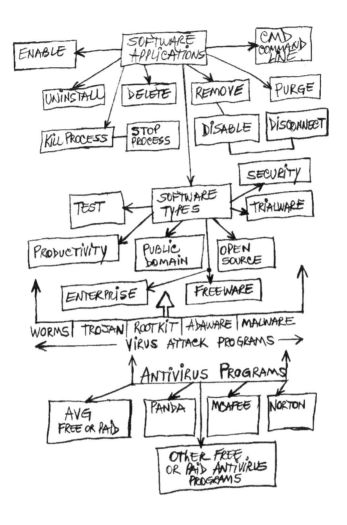

ENABLE ← SOFTWARE APPLICATIONS → CMD COMMAND LINE

UNINSTALL   DELETE   REMOVE   PURGE

KILL PROCESS   STOP PROCESS   DISABLE   DISCONNECT

TEST ← SOFTWARE TYPES → SECURITY   TRIALWARE

PRODUCTIVITY   PUBLIC DOMAIN   OPEN SOURCE

ENTERPRISE   FREEWARE

WORMS | TROJAN | ROOTKIT | ADAWARE | MALWARE

← VIRUS ATTACK PROGRAMS →

ANTIVIRUS PROGRAMS

AVG FREE OR PAID   PANDA   MCAFEE   NORTON

OTHER FREE, OR PAID ANTIVIRUS PROGRAMS

2016 COPYRIGHT ⓒ ALFONSO J. KINGLOW

10

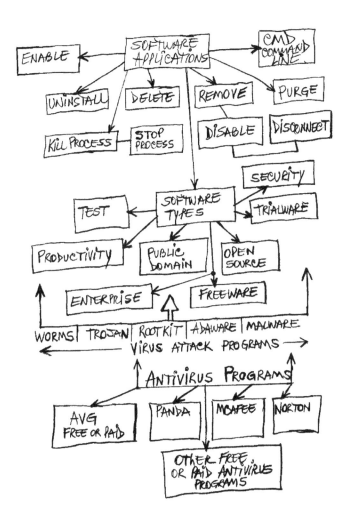

ENABLE ← SOFTWARE APPLICATIONS → CMD COMMAND LINE

SOFTWARE APPLICATIONS → UNINSTALL, DELETE, REMOVE, PURGE

KILL PROCESS, STOP PROCESS

REMOVE → DISABLE, DISCONNECT

SOFTWARE TYPES → TEST, SECURITY, TRIALWARE

PRODUCTIVITY, PUBLIC DOMAIN, OPEN SOURCE

ENTERPRISE, FREEWARE

WORMS | TROJAN | ROOTKIT | ADAWARE | MALWARE

VIRUS ATTACK PROGRAMS →

ANTIVIRUS PROGRAMS

AVG FREE OR PAID, PANDA, MCAFEE, NORTON

OTHER FREE OR PAID ANTIVIRUS PROGRAMS

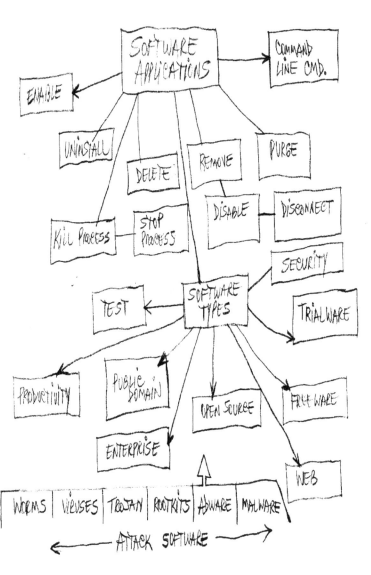

SOFTWARE APPLICATIONS

COMMAND LINE CMD.

ENABLE

UNINSTALL

DELETE

REMOVE

PURGE

DISABLE

DISCONNECT

KILL PROCESS

STOP PROCESS

SECURITY

TEST

SOFTWARE TYPES

TRIALWARE

PRODUCTIVITY

PUBLIC DOMAIN

OPEN SOURCE

FREE WARE

ENTERPRISE

WEB

| WORMS | VIRUSES | TROJAN | ROOTKITS | ADWARE | MALWARE |

← ATTACK SOFTWARE →

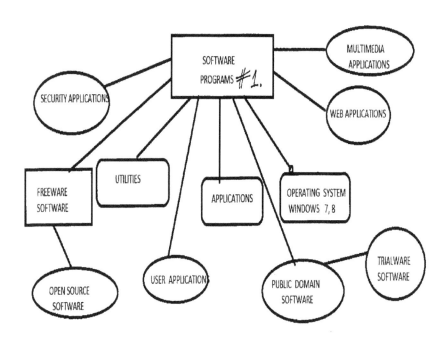

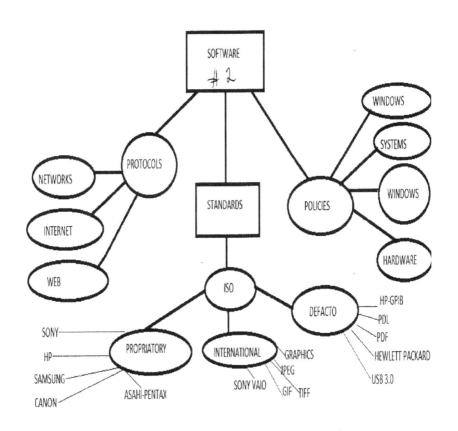

SOFTWARE
2

PROTOCOLS

NETWORKS

INTERNET

WEB

STANDARDS

POLICIES

WINDOWS

SYSTEMS

WINDOWS

HARDWARE

ISO

DEFACTO

HP-GPIB
PDL
PDF
HEWLETT PACKARD
USB 3.0

SONY
HP
SAMSUNG
CANON
ASAHI-PENTAX

PROPRIATORY

INTERNATIONAL

GRAPHICS
JPEG
SONY VAIO
GIF TIFF

SEARCH ENGINES

INTERNET

APPLICATION SOFTWARE

FERRET

GOOGLE
EXCITE
HOTBOT
LYCOS
YAHOO
ALTAVISTA
LOOKSMART
WEBCRAWLER

PORTAL

BRIDGE

MULTIMEDIA WEB PAGE

ANIMATION

GRAPHICS FORMATS

BMP. BIT MAP
GIF. GRAPHICS INTERCHANGE FORMAT
JPEG. JOINT PHOTOGRAPHIC EXPERTS
                    GROUP.
PCX. PC PAINTBRUSH
PNG. PORTABLE NETWORK GRAPHICS
TIFF. TAGGED IMAGE FILE FORMAT

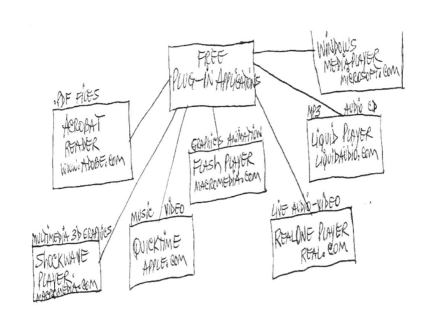

FREE
PLUG-IN APPLICATIONS

WINDOWS
MEDIA PLAYER
MICROSOFT. COM

.PDF FILES
ACROBAT
READER
WWW.ADOBE.COM

MP3   AUDIO CD
LIQUID PLAYER
LIQUIDAUDIO. COM

GRAPHICS ANIMATION
FLASH PLAYER
MACROMEDIA.COM

MUSIC / VIDEO
QUICKTIME
APPLE. COM

LIVE AUDIO-VIDEO
REALONE PLAYER
REAL. COM

MULTIMEDIA 3D GRAPHICS
SHOCKWAVE
PLAYER.
MACROMEDIA.COM

* EXTEND THE CAPABILITY OF YOUR
BROWSER BY INSTALLING A PLUG-IN
TO DISPLAY MULTIMEDIA ELEMENTS.

MACHINE AND HUMAN BASIC INFORMATION PROCESS.—

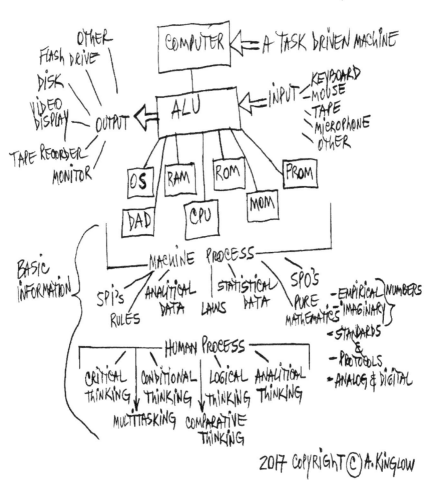

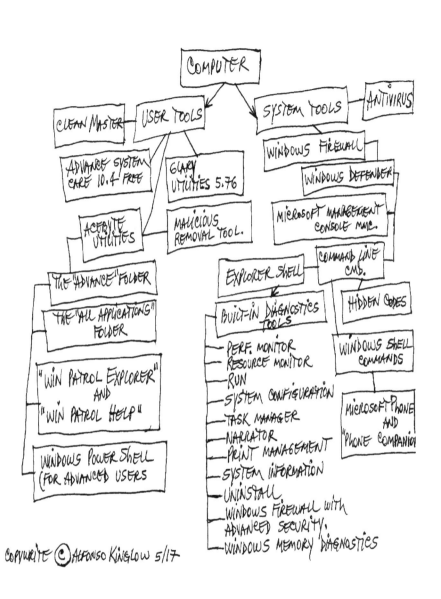

COMPUTER

USER TOOLS

SYSTEM TOOLS

ANTIVIRUS

CLEAN MASTER

ADVANCE SYSTEM CARE 10.4 FREE

GLARY UTILITIES 5.76

ACEBYTE UTILITIES

MALICIOUS REMOVAL TOOL.

WINDOWS FIREWALL

WINDOWS DEFENDER

MICROSOFT MANAGEMENT CONSOLE MMC.

THE "ADVANCE" FOLDER

THE "ALL APPLICATIONS" FOLDER

"WIN PATROL EXPLORER" AND "WIN PATROL HELP"

WINDOWS POWER SHELL (FOR ADVANCED USERS

EXPLORER SHELL

COMMAND LINE CMD.

BUILT-IN DIAGNOSTICS TOOLS

HIDDEN CODES

- PERF. MONITOR
- RESOURCE MONITOR
- RUN
- SYSTEM CONFIGURATION
- TASK MANAGER
- NARRATOR
- PRINT MANAGEMENT
- SYSTEM INFORMATION
- UNINSTALL
- WINDOWS FIREWALL WITH ADVANCED SECURITY.
- WINDOWS MEMORY DIAGNOSTICS

WINDOWS SHELL COMMANDS

MICROSOFT PHONE AND "PHONE COMPANION

COPYWRITE © ALFONSO KINGLOW 5/17

COMPUTERS

↓

TASK DRIVEN MACHINES

↓

MULTI-TASKING MACHINES

↓

COMPUTERS SPEAK THEIR OWN LANGUAGE

↓

THE COMPUTER LANGUAGE IS A BINARY LANGUAGE THAT REPRESENT ZERO (∅) AND ONE (1) AND IS DIGITAL.

↓

THE COMPUTER LANGUAGE IS CALLED A (BIT) OR BINARY LANGUAGE, AND IS THE SMALLEST UNIT OF INFORMATION THAT CAN BE TRANSMITTED OR RECEIVED.

↓

BECAUSE THE "BIT" IS VERY SMALL, IT IS DIVIDED INTO GROUPS OF 8. (∅-1-∅-1-1-∅-∅-1) THAT IS CALLED A "BYTE." (8 BITS = 1 BYTE).

↓

"BYTES" ARE STILL TOO SMALL, AND WAS DIVIDED INTO A GROUP OF 8, IN ORDER TO TRANSMIT/RECEIVE A "WORD." (8 BYTES = 1 WORD).

? HOW MANY ZERO'S (∅) AND 1'S ARE IN ONE WORD?

COMPUTERS
(CONTINUING)

BECAUSE COMPUTERS USE THEIR OWN LANGUAGE (BINARY); THEY NEED A "TRANSLATOR."

IN ORDER TO TRANSMIT LARGE AMOUNTS OF "WORDS," CALLED "DATA"; THE METRIC SYSTEM IS USED, CALLED: "KILO"=1000, "MEGA"= MILLION, "GIGA" OR BILLION AND "TERA"= TRILLION

ONE THOUSAND BYTES IS = 1 KB OR ONE KILOBYTE.
ONE MILLION BYTES IS = 1 MB OR ONE MEGABYTES.
ONE BILLION BYTES IS = 1 GB OR ONE BILLION
ONE TRILLION BYTES IS = 1 TB OR ONE TRILLION BYTES.

COMPUTER "MEMORY" CALLED "RAM" RANDOM ACCESS MEMORY WAS DIVIDED INTO 1GB-2GB-4GB-8GB-16GB 32GB-64GB-128GB.

COMPUTER "STORAGE" OR HARD DRIVE WAS DIVIDED INTO 250 GB.- 500 GB.-1TB - 1.5TB AND MORE...

COPYRIGHT © ALFONSO KINGLOW 2017

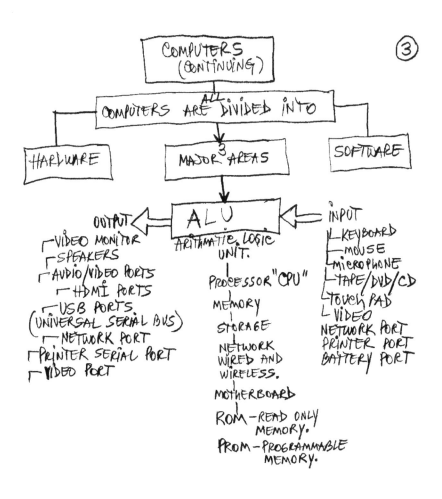

COMPUTERS
(CONTINUING)

③

COMPUTERS ARE ALL DIVIDED INTO

HARDWARE

MAJOR 3 AREAS

SOFTWARE

OUTPUT ← ALU ← INPUT
ARITHMATIC LOGIC UNIT.

OUTPUT:
- VIDEO MONITOR
- SPEAKERS
- AUDIO/VIDEO PORTS
- HDMI PORTS
- USB PORTS. (UNIVERSAL SERIAL BUS)
- NETWORK PORT
- PRINTER SERIAL PORT
- VIDEO PORT

PROCESSOR "CPU"

MEMORY
|
STORAGE

NETWORK
WIRED AND
WIRELESS.

MOTHERBOARD
|
ROM — READ ONLY
MEMORY.

PROM — PROGRAMMABLE
MEMORY.

INPUT:
- KEYBOARD
- MOUSE
- MICROPHONE
- TAPE/DVD/CD
- TOUCH PAD
- VIDEO
NETWORK PORT
PRINTER PORT
BATTERY PORT

COMPUTERS
(CONTINUING)

THE CENTRAL PROCESSING UNIT
OR CPU. "THE COMPUTER HEART."

THE SPEED OF THE COMPUTER PROCESSOR "CPU"
IS MEASURED IN "CYCLES" OR HERTZ.
1 HERTZ (1 hz.) = 1 CYCLE PER SECOND (CPS.)

THE MINIMUM "CPU" SPEED SHOULD BE 2.5 Ghz.
OR 2.5 GIGAHERTZ. A FAST COMPUTER WILL
HAVE A PROCESSOR OF 2.8 Ghz OR 3.0 Ghz OR
HIGHER. PROCESSORS ARE SINGLE-CORE, DUAL
CORE OR QUAD-CORE.

"INTEL" IS THE LARGEST MANUFACTURER OF PROCESSORS
IN THE WORLD, FOLLOWED BY AMD, MOTOROLA AND
IBM. THE "INTEL" XEON, QUAD-CORE, i-7,
i-8, i-9 AND BEYOND, ARE THE FASTEST
PROCESSORS (CPU) IN THE WORLD., AND ARE
RATED AT 3.5 Ghz. SPEED, AND BEYOND...

* SEE MINIMUM HARDWARE REQUIREMENTS...

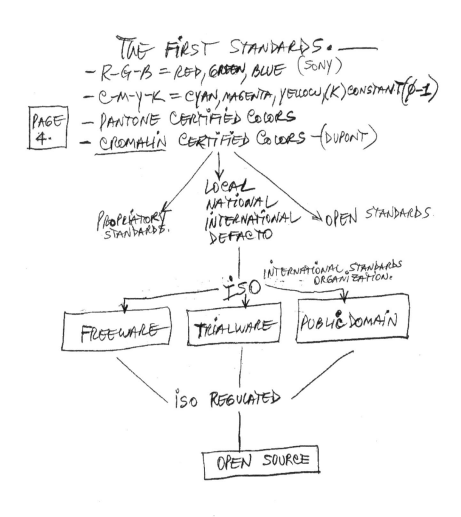

THE FIRST STANDARDS. ——
- R-G-B = RED, GREEN, BLUE (SONY)
- C-M-Y-K = CYAN, MAGENTA, YELLOW, (K) CONSTANT ($0-1$)
PAGE 4. - PANTONE CERTIFIED COLORS
- CROMALIN CERTIFIED COLORS (DUPONT)

PROPRIETARY STANDARDS.

LOCAL
NATIONAL
INTERNATIONAL
DEFACTO

OPEN STANDARDS.

ISO   INTERNATIONAL STANDARDS ORGANIZATION.

FREEWARE   TRIALWARE   PUBLIC DOMAIN

ISO REGULATED

OPEN SOURCE

This is not the **End.**

WRITE HERE

WRITE HERE

WRITE HERE

WRITE HERE

AUTHOR NAME

WRITE   HERE

WRITE HERE

END. 74 PAGES.

www.ingramcontent.com/pod-product-compliance
Lightning Source LLC
Chambersburg PA
CBHW070838070326
40690CB00009B/1606